Camouflage

Phil Gates

CAMBRIDGE
UNIVERSITY PRESS

Cambridge Reading

General Editors
Richard Brown and Kate Ruttle

Consultant Editor
Jean Glasberg

PUBLISHED BY THE PRESS SYNDICATE OF THE UNIVERSITY OF CAMBRIDGE
The Pitt Building, Trumpington Street, Cambridge CB2 1RP, United Kingdom

CAMBRIDGE UNIVERSITY PRESS
The Edinburgh Building, Cambridge CB2 2RU, United Kingdom
40 West 20th Street, New York, NY 10011-4211, USA
10 Stamford Road, Oakleigh, Melbourne 3166, Australia

First published 1997
Third printing 1998

Printed in the United Kingdom at the University Press, Cambridge

Typeset in Concorde and Franklin Gothic

A catalogue record for this book is available from the British Library

ISBN 0 521 49967 4 paperback

Picture research: Callie Kendall

Acknowledgements
We are grateful to the following for permission to reproduce photographs:

Front cover: Tony Stone Images (photo: © David E Myers)
Back cover: Tony Stone Images (photo: © Tim Davis)

Bryan & Cherry Alexander: 14*t*, 14 *heading*, 24*c*

BBC Natural History Unit Picture Library:
1, © Gerry Ellis; 14*br*, © Thomas D Mangelsen

Phil Gates: 19*cl*, 19*cr*

ICCE Photolibrary:
21 *heading*, 22, 24*l*, © David Illiff

Oxford Scientific Films:
4*tl*, © J S & E J Woolmer; 4*tr*, © Bob Fredrick; 4*bl*, © Leonard Lee Rue III/Animals Animals;
4*br*, © D G Fox; 5*tl*, © P & W Ward; 5*tr*, © Max Gibbs; 5*bl*, © Max Gibbs; 5*br(t)*, © Harry Taylor;
5*br(b)*, © Peter O'Toole; 6*t*, © Mills Tandy; 6*c*, © Mark Hamblin; 6*b*, © J A L Cooke; 7*t*, © Anna Walsh;
7*b*, © Peter Parks; 10*t*, © Breck P Kent/Animals Animals; 10*bl*, © Peter Parks; 10*br*, © G I Bernard;
11*t*, © Paul Kay; 11*c*, © David B Fleetham; 14*bl*, © Press-Tige Pictures; 15*tl*, © Tom McHugh/Photo
Researchers Inc.; 15*tr*, © Brock May/Photo Researchers Inc.; 15*cl*, 24*b*, © E R Degginger/Animals
Animals; 15*cr*, © N Rosing/Okapia; 15*b*, © Michael W Richards; 18*t*, © Stan Osolinski; 18*cl*,
18 *heading*, © Derek Bromhall; 18*cr*, © Ray Coleman/Photo Researchers Inc.; 18*bl*, © Densey
Clyne/Mantis Wildlife Films; 18*br*, © Michael Fogden; 19*t*, 19 *heading*, 24*r*, © K G Vock/Okapia;
19*b*, © P & W Ward; 20, © Max Gibbs

K Wheeler: 11*b*, 21

Contents

Ways of hiding

Some animals use their colour and shape to help them hide and keep safe from danger. This way of hiding is called camouflage.

← A comma butterfly looks like a dead leaf when its wings are folded.

But when its → wings are open, it looks quite different!

This grasshopper has a thin, green body and thin, green legs that help it to hide in the grass.

↑ Snowshoe hares are white, like the snow.

It is difficult for other →
animals to see the shape
of this angel fish because
of its bright stripes.

When crab spiders keep still,
it is difficult to see them.
↓

These Indian glass fish have
no colour at all – you can see
through them. This is one of the
ways that sea animals can hide.
↓

This harmless
hover-fly looks
very like a wasp. →
The wasp has a
dangerous sting.

This toad is hard to see because its skin is the same colour as the dead leaves. →

← A woodcock builds its nest among dead leaves. The colours of the woodcock's feathers are the same as the colours of the leaves. This means that when a woodcock is sitting on its nest, it is almost invisible.

When a looper caterpillar is in → danger it keeps quite still. Its shape and colour make it look like a dead twig, so hungry birds cannot see it easily.

When a mother red deer goes to look for food, she has to leave her fawn behind.

The markings on the fawn's coat look like dappled sunlight. This makes it difficult to see the fawn when it sits in the long grass.

Can you see the moth on this tree trunk?
It is very hard to find the moth because the pattern on its wings is the same as the pattern on the tree trunk.

There are twelve animals in this wood hidden by their camouflage. Can you find them all?

Hiding under the sea

Flatfish have flat bodies that do not make a shadow when they are lying on the sea bed.

Flatfish can also change the patterns on their skin to match colours on the sea bed. This makes it even harder to spot them.

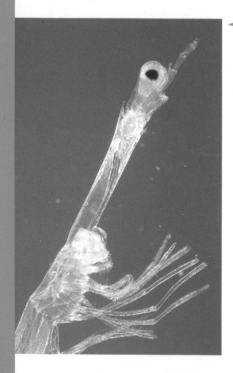

Some prawns and shrimps have no colour at all. You can see right through them and this makes them nearly invisible in the water.

A rock goby is a little fish. Its skin has the same colours and patterns as the sand on the bottom of a rock pool.

Spider crabs stick little pieces of seaweed onto their legs and shell. They use this camouflage to help them hide among the seaweed in rock-pools.

Hermit crabs live inside old seashells. The shells protect the crabs from other animals. The hermit crabs pick up sea anemones and stick them onto their shells – a camouflaged shell is an even better hiding place.

These little snails are called periwinkles. They are difficult to find because their shells are the same colours as the seaweeds that they are eating.

There are twelve camouflaged animals hidden in this rock pool on the seashore. Can you find them all?

Hiding in the snow

The white fur of a polar bear camouflages it against the ice and snow in the Arctic. →

← This animal is called a stoat. In winter, the colour of its coat changes from brown to white, and it is almost invisible against the snow. Only the tip of its tail stays black.

↓

This animal is called a lemming. Its coat turns white in winter and matches the colour of the snow.

Arctic hares have white fur in winter. When they sit in the snow they are difficult to see.

A snowy owl is almost as white as snow. In winter, it is difficult for other animals to see the owl swooping down to catch them.

This little bird is called a snow bunting. Its feathers are white, so it is hidden against the snow.

Snow geese have white feathers. This makes it very hard to see snow geese when they land in the snow.

There are twelve camouflaged
animals hidden in the snow.
Can you find them all?

This bird is called a bittern. It lives in reed beds beside lakes. When it is frightened, it sticks its beak straight up in the air and stands still. Then its shape and colour match the reeds.

This crab spider eats butterflies. It sits perfectly still inside a flower and its colour matches the petals. Butterflies do not see the spider, so they land on the flower and the spider catches them.

This long, thin stick insect is the same colour as a twig. This makes it very hard to find the stick insect when it stands still on a plant.

The flower mantis eats butterflies too. Its legs and body look just like a flower.

Thorn bugs are insects that look like rose prickles. To hide from danger they line up along a plant stem and keep perfectly still, so they look like thorns.

Pretending to be dangerous

Harmless animals that look like dangerous animals are called mimics.

Wasps do not need to → hide because they can defend themselves with a painful sting.
  Other insects that do not have a sting often mimic wasps. The yellow-and-black markings warn other animals to keep away.

Hover-flies look like dangerous wasps, but they ← are harmless.

← This beetle is yellow and black, like a wasp. It does not have a sting, but other animals take warning from its wasp-like markings and leave it alone.

There are a lot of animals and birds → that eat moths. They are the moths' predators. This moth looks like a wasp. It does not have a sting, but predators leave it alone because they think it is dangerous.

19

Bright colours and patterns

Sometimes animals use bright colours and patterns to confuse their predators.

Predators usually try to grab their prey by the head.

These butterfly fish have a spot near their tails that looks like an eye. This confuses predators, as they cannot tell which part of the butterfly fish is its head and which is the tail.

Sometimes butterfly fish swim slowly backwards, so their tails look even more like heads.

And if camouflage fails . . .

Sometimes camouflage can help animals to play a trick on their enemies and frighten them away.

A peacock butterfly rests with its wings folded. The pattern on the underside of its wings camouflages it, so that it looks just like a dead leaf.

Usually this camouflage works, but sometimes it fails and a bird finds the peacock butterfly. When that happens, the butterfly quickly . . .

. . . opens its wings!

The butterfly's wings have patterns that look like four giant eyes. The bird is so frightened that it flies away, and the butterfly can escape.

Glossary

Arctic the area of ice and snow around the North Pole

camouflage a kind of disguise, where the colour and shape of an animal make it difficult to see

confuse make it difficult to understand something or see something clearly

dappled a pattern of light and dark colours, like the patches of sunshine and shadow under a tree

defend protect from danger

fawn a young deer

invisible Something that is *invisible* cannot be seen.

mimic an animal that copies the way that a different animal looks or behaves

pattern An animal's colours or markings can make up a *pattern* – a tiger's stripes, for example.

predator an animal that hunts other animals

prey animals that are hunted by predators

reed a tall grass. A **reed bed** is a place where lots of reeds grow close together.

Animals hidden in the wood *(pages 8–9)*	**Animals hidden in the rock pool** *(pages 12–13)*	**Animals hidden in the snow** *(pages 16–17)*
four moths	octopus	snowy owl
two caterpillars	spider crab	Arctic hare
woodcock	hermit crab	polar bear
nightjar	two rock gobies	Arctic fox
fawn	flatfish	lemming
tawny owl	red periwinkle	stoat
pheasant	brown periwinkle	baby seal
squirrel	two green periwinkles	two snow geese
	prawn	two snow buntings
	sea urchin	reindeer

Index